Comments pertaining to this report are invited and should be forwarded to: Director, Strategic Studies Institute and U.S. Army War College Press, U.S. Army War College, 47 Ashburn Drive, Carlisle, PA 17013-5010.

This manuscript was funded by the U.S. Army War College External Research Associates Program. Information on this program is available on our website, *www.StrategicStudies Institute.army.mil*, at the Opportunities tab.

The Strategic Studies Institute and U.S. Army War College Press publishes a monthly email newsletter to update the national security community on the research of our analysts, recent and forthcoming publications, and upcoming conferences sponsored by the Institute. Each newsletter also provides a strategic commentary by one of our research analysts. If you are interested in receiving this newsletter, please subscribe on the SSI website at *www.StrategicStudiesInstitute.army.mil/newsletter*.

The authors gratefully acknowledge the contributions of Lieutenant Colonel Chris Danbeck, former 2nd Brigade Combat

Team/1st Infantry Division S3; and Mr. Mike Knippel, Forces Command Regionally Aligned Forces Staff Integrator.

*****

Monographs in the "Officer Talent Management Series☐ (2009-10) include:

1. *Towards a U.S. Army Officer Corps Strategy for Success: A Proposed Human Capital Model Focused upon Talent,* March 31, 2009.
2. *Talent: Implications for a U.S. Army Officer Corps Strategy,* October 28, 2009.
3. *Towards a U.S. Army Officer Corps Strategy for Success: Retaining Talent,* January 15, 2010.
4. *Accessing Talent: The Foundation of a U.S. Army Officer Corps Strategy,* February 19, 2010.
5. *Towards a U.S. Army Officer Corps Strategy for Success: Developing Talent,* March 29, 2010.
6. *Towards a U.S. Army Officer Corps Strategy for Success: Employing Talent,* May 5, 2010.

The United States Army War College

The United States Army War College educates and develops leaders for service at the strategic level while advancing knowledge in the global application of Landpower.

The purpose of the United States Army War College is to produce graduates who are skilled critical thinkers and complex problem solvers. Concurrently, it is our duty to the U.S. Army to also act as a ⬜think factory⬜for commanders and civilian leaders at the strategic level worldwide and routinely engage in discourse and debate concerning the role of ground forces in achieving national security objectives.

The Strategic Studies Institute publishes national security and strategic research and analysis to influence policy debate and bridge the gap between military and academia.

The Center for Strategic Leadership and Development contributes to the education of world class senior leaders, develops expert knowledge, and provides solutions to strategic Army issues affecting the national security community.

The Peacekeeping and Stability Operations Institute provides subject matter expertise, technical review, and writing expertise to agencies that develop stability operations concepts and doctrines.

U.S. Army War College

Senior Leader Development and Resiliency

The Senior Leader Development and Resiliency program supports the United States Army War College⬜s lines of effort to educate strategic leaders and provide well-being education and support by developing self-awareness through leader feedback and leader resiliency.

The School of Strategic Landpower develops strategic leaders by providing a strong foundation of wisdom grounded in mastery of the profession of arms, and by serving as a crucible for educating future leaders in the analysis, evaluation, and refinement of professional expertise in war, strategy, operations, national security, resource management, and responsible command.

The U.S. Army Heritage and Education Center acquires, conserves, and exhibits historical materials for use to support the U.S. Army, educate an international audience, and honor Soldiers⬜ past and present.

STRATEGIC STUDIES INSTITUTE

The Strategic Studies Institute (SSI) is part of the U.S. Army War College and is the strategic-level study agent for issues related to national security and military strategy with emphasis on geostrategic analysis.

The mission of SSI is to use independent analysis to conduct strategic studies that develop policy recommendations on:

- Strategy, planning, and policy for joint and combined employment of military forces;

- Regional strategic appraisals;

- The nature of land warfare;

- Matters affecting the Army's future;

- The concepts, philosophy, and theory of strategy; and,

- Other issues of importance to the leadership of the Army.

Studies produced by civilian and military analysts concern topics having strategic implications for the Army, the Department of Defense, and the larger national security community.

In addition to its studies, SSI publishes special reports on topics of special or immediate interest. These include edited proceedings of conferences and topically oriented roundtables, expanded trip reports, and quick-reaction responses to senior Army leaders.

The Institute provides a valuable analytical capability within the Army to address strategic and other issues in support of Army participation in national security policy formulation.

Strategic Studies Institute
and
U.S. Army War College Press

CREATING AN EFFECTIVE REGIONAL ALIGNMENT STRATEGY FOR THE U.S. ARMY

Raven Bukowski
John Childress
Michael J. Colarusso
David S. Lyle

November 2014

FOREWORD

This monograph focuses upon ⬚regional alignment,⬚ viewed by many as critical if the Army is to remain both relevant and effective in the 21st century security environment. Despite its title, the monograph is part of the Strategic Studies Institute⬚s ongoing ⬚talent management⬚ series. In fact, the authors argue that world class talent management is a necessary precondition to creating an effective regional alignment strategy for the Army. They identify several serious challenges to creating a workable regional alignment of Army units, most of which hinge upon understanding and liberating the unique talents of individual soldiers and civilians. They also argue that the Army⬚s current Force Generation Model is not conducive to creating and maintaining regionally expert units and must be adjusted accordingly.

As the Army⬚s most senior leaders are focused upon regional alignment to maximize unit effectiveness in a time of fiscal austerity and global uncertainty, the ideas discussed in this monograph merit close attention.

DOUGLAS C. LOVELACE, JR.
Director
Strategic Studies Institute and
    U.S. Army War College Press

ABOUT THE AUTHORS

MAJOR RAVEN BUKOWSKI is an Assistant Professor of International Relations at the United States Military Academy, West Point, NY. Her research interests include civil-military relations, near-peer strategic culture, intelligence policy, and security and development strategies for countries in transition. Major Bukowski holds a B.S. from West Point and an M.A. in international economics and strategic studies from the Johns Hopkins School of Advanced International Studies.

MAJOR JOHN CHILDRESS is an Assistant Professor of American Politics and a member of the U.S. Army's Office of Economic and Manpower Analysis at the United States Military Academy, West Point, NY. His research interests include reforms to the Army Human Resources employment model, Veterans' Affairs, and Grand Strategy. Major Childress holds a B.S. from West Point and an M.A. in public policy from the Georgetown Public Policy Institute.

LIEUTENANT COLONEL (RET.) MICHAEL J. COLARUSSO is a Senior Research Analyst in the Army's Office of Economic and Manpower Analysis at the United States Military Academy, West Point. Lieutenant Colonel Colarusso recently co-authored "Senior Officer Talent Management: Fostering Institutional Adaptability," published by the U.S. Army War College's Strategic Studies Institute (SSI) (2014). His previous SSI publications include the monograph series "Officer Talent Management Series" (2009-10). His primary areas of research are organizational design, generational dynamics, human capital, and talent management. Lieutenant Colonel Colarusso holds a B.A. in history from Saint John's University and an M.A. in history from the Pennsylvania State University.

LIEUTENANT COLONEL DAVID S. LYLE is an Associate Professor of Economics and Director of the Army's Office of Economic and Manpower Analysis at the United States Military Academy, West Point, NY. His primary areas of research are labor economics, econometrics, human capital, and talent management. Lieutenant Colonel Lyle has published articles in the *Journal of Political Economy*, the *Journal of Labor Economics*, the *Review of Economics and Statistics*, the *American Economic Journal: Applied*, the *Economics of Education Review*, and the *American Economic Association*. He also co-authored "Senior Officer Talent Management: Fostering Institutional Adaptability," published by SSI of the U.S. Army War College (2014). His previous SSI publications include the monograph series "Officer Talent Management Series" (2009-10). Lieutenant Colonel Lyle holds a B.S. from West Point and a Ph.D. in economics from the Massachusetts Institute of Technology.

SUMMARY

As the war in Afghanistan draws to a close, the U.S. Army is increasingly focused upon ⸋regionally aligning⸋ its forces. To do so effectively, however, it must undertake several initiatives. First, the Army must acknowledge and liberate the unique productive capabilities (talents) of each individual. Second, it must shift from process-oriented, industrial age personnel management to productivity-focused, information age talent management. Third, the Army must foster enduring human relationships between its organizations and the governments, militaries, and populations to which they are regionally aligned. Hand in hand with this, it must redesign its Force Generation Model to create regional expertise at both individual and organizational levels. Fourth, the Army must ensure that regional alignment does not degrade the worldwide "flex" capabilities of its forces.

CREATING AN EFFECTIVE REGIONAL ALIGNMENT STRATEGY FOR THE U.S. ARMY

INTRODUCTION

Sometimes past is prologue. So it is with "regional alignment," a centerpiece of the U.S. Army's emerging strategy. In a way, it echoes Cold War practices, when Army units were habitually aligned to differing theaters, immersed in local politics and culture, and trained and equipped to meet specific regional threats.[1] While this experience certainly provides invaluable insights for future regional alignment planning, 21st century threats demand a significantly modified approach.

As Chief of Staff General Raymond Odierno wrote in 2012, "We've learned many lessons over the last 10 years, but one of the most compelling is that . . . nothing is as important to [our] long-term success as understanding the prevailing culture and values of areas in which the Army may operate.[2] The Army's 2013 *Strategic Planning Guidance* contains similar themes, highlighting that " . . . success depends as much on understanding the *social* and *political* fabric of the situation as it does on the ability to physically dominate it."[3] Other official pronouncements express similar sentiments. For example, *Army.mil* recently ran a U.S. Army Central (ARCENT) Command story proclaiming " . . . the Future Hinges on Regional Alignments."[4]

Clearly, the Army's leadership believes that regionally aligned, culturally fluent forces will improve its ability to "prevent, shape, and win" as part of the larger joint force.[5] Because the concept departs from the "plug and play," modular deployment approach of the last decade, it has generated significant defense media attention.[6] In 2012, for example, *Stripes.com* reported "AFRICOM [U.S. Africa Command] First to Test New Regional Brigade Concept."[7] In October 2013, *Defensenews.com* announced "New Training to Focus on Regionally Aligned Forces Concept,"[8] followed closely by an *Army Times* piece which theorized that "Regional Alignment May Boost Soldiers'Career Stability."[9] Professional journal articles have also proliferated in the last 2 years, with pundits both inside and outside of the defense establishment weighing in on the topic.

Yet despite talk about regional alignment, the Army has taken few concrete steps to prepare for this dramatic change. While enormous in its implications, the Army's current regional alignment plan seems to be little more than directing units to "focus regionally" and aligning them with the appropriate combatant command. While regionally tailored equipment packages and deeper relationships with local allies are likely to follow, creating formations with the expertise to dominate in regional missions is a far larger challenge—a human capital one.

Over the past decade, the Army has slowly recognized the need to change its people policies. Perhaps no clearer acknowledgment exists than that found in the current *Army Capstone Concept*, which calls for the Army to ". . . refine its accessions processes to attract, select and place people in ways that match talents and skills to the tasks of any given specialty."[10] It also states that the Army must manage and apply talent more effectively to maximize individual potential and emphasize the value and necessity of investment in the Army's most valuable resource: its soldiers and civilians.[11]

Despite this, current Army personnel practices remain rooted in an industrial age approach that fails to recognize the unique productive capabilities that each soldier or civilian brings to the force. Perhaps even more problematic, the Army has no mechanism to identify relevant regional talents or experiences such as cultural fluencies, foreign contacts, or travel abroad. Nor can it identify which duties or assignments demand more regional expertise than others. Without this information, the Army is unable to match soldier talents with the demand for them. Today's rigid personnel management system continues to prioritize assignment requirements over individual qualifications and standardized career timelines over unit readiness. This will surely prevent regionally aligned units from reaching their optimal operational capabilities.

These challenges are not the fault of any individual soldier, officer, or command. Army Human Resources Command (HRC) professionals work tirelessly to meet the Army's needs, but they are trapped in an outmoded human resources (HR) system that prevents them from managing talent most effectively. To succeed in regional alignment (or in any strategic endeavor, for that matter), the Army must redesign its human capital management system for the 21st century. Of course, changing personnel policy is tough for any organization, particularly a large, tradition-focused bureaucracy bound by the sinewy muscles of time-worn practices.

Historically, the greatest shifts in Army HR management have coincided with force expansion or drawdown, much like that occurring today. This is why now is exactly the right time to adopt a talent management approach in the Army's human capital domain. Without it, talk of genuine regional alignment will remain just that☐ talk. Although organizational and equipment tables may be rewritten, genuinely enhanced regional capabilities will remain elusive.

It doesn☐t have to be this way. Five talent management and organizational design imperatives can make effective regional alignment a reality. The Army must: acknowledge and liberate the unique productive capabilities (talents) of each individual; shift from process-oriented, industrial age personnel management to productivity-focused, information age talent management; create enduring human relationships between regionally aligned organizations and their target nations, populations, and defense establishments; redesign its Force Generation (ARFORGEN) Model to provide the stability and tenure needed to foster deep regional expertise at both the individual and organizational levels; and maintain the global "flex" capabilities of regionally aligned units.

Acknowledge and Liberate the Unique Talents of Each Individual.

Every person has a particular talent distribution☐ a unique intersection of skills, knowledge, and behaviors that create optimal levels of performance, provided that person is employed against jobs that liberate his or her particular talents.[12] Unfortunately, the Army☐s current personnel system is unable to align talents against work requirements because it has an incomplete picture of both. Essentially, the Army employs a two-dimensional approach to HR management, assigning individuals on the basis of functional specialty (branch or career field) and years of service (☐time in grade,☐ or rank).[13] Additionally, each job has a generic description such as ☐company commander☐or ☐squad leader,☐denoting little about the position☐s actual work demands. Such ambiguity forces the Army☐s personnel system to treat people as interchangeable parts. This prevents optimal employment, stymies professional growth, and hampers unit productivity.

Consider Paul, for example, a Military Intelligence (MI) officer fluent in Mandarin Chinese and possessing a top tier Master☐s Degree in Economics and Southeast Asia Studies. Having developed his language skills and regional expertise through the Army☐s Advanced Civil Schooling (ACS) graduate school program, Paul continued to deepen his fluency after school through self-study. Not only does he possess broad **intelligence** expertise, he has developed deep **regional** expertise via the Army☐s investment in him. Unfortunately, the investment was squandered when the current personnel management system assigned Paul to a 3-year recruiting command position in Ohio.[14]

This example is not meant to suggest that every Chinese speaking officer should be permanently posted to Southeast Asia. A truly regionally focused Army, however, should have at least **considered** Paul☐s suitability for Pacific theater service. Today's personnel management system cannot do so, however, because it lacks both the information and policies necessary. It does not know the specifics of Paul's graduate studies, only that he has a Master☐s degree. It cannot see his self-study and resultant deep fluencies, so Paul is instead managed as an interchangeable part, available for reassignment to any intelligence or ☐branch immaterial☐vacancy requiring his pay grade. What is more, the significant taxpayer investments made in Paul's education may be lost if his regional expertise deteriorates in Cleveland or if he is poached from the Army by a more insightful employer.[15]

In contrast, an information age, talent management approach leverages the unique talents of each person to improve organizational performance. True talent management rejects the notion of □talent□as the □top 5 or 10 percent,□an elitist approach that manages a tiny fraction of the workforce while neglecting the development and employment of the majority. There are limitless dimensions and distributions of talent, and **every** person possesses a unique set of both.[16] When an employer acknowledges this, it can begin to effectively manage its **entire** labor force, maximizing productivity, development, worker satisfaction, and retention.

These are worthy outcomes to pursue in today's fiscally austere defense environment. Instead of repeatedly missing the chance to leverage its own human capital investments, a talent management approach will allow the Army to better □manage, train, and develop soldiers to support regional alignment . . .□ in accordance with the leadership□s vision.[17] It will capture the regional expertise a soldier possesses or gains from experiences both inside **and** outside of the Army.

Adopt Information Age Talent Management Practices.

With the right data, supporting policies, and robust information management systems, the Army can more effectively manage soldier talents across the full spectrum of land-combat demands. Whether the future fight is conventional, shifts towards space and cyber, or demands the newest warfighting function of □engagement,□talent management can align the right expertise against any challenge and at minimal cost.[18]

Even during the heyday of Cold War regional alignment, however, the Army failed to leverage the abundant expertise present in its labor force. Although the Army has maintained a regional focus on the Korean Peninsula for over 60 years, its personnel management policies have remained inimical to the accession, retention, development, or employment of regional expertise. For example, only 27 percent of all soldiers assigned to Korea in the 1990s ever returned for a follow-up assignment.[19] Rapid personnel churn in the name of tour ⊡equity⊡exacerbates the problem, degrading cultural fluency and personal relationships with allies while creating cyclical gaps in the institutional knowledge of forward deployed units.[20] The Army must do more than apply its Cold War, Korean model of regional alignment to the rest of the force. It must develop and align the right talents to each region.

Army Special Forces (SF) already practice much of this approach. Its regionally focused units employ a systematic procedure for evaluating candidates against job-related dimensions that are specific to the Special Forces Group and the operational environments in which they serve.[21] For example, the regional expertise of each SF candidate is evaluated via tools such as the Defense Language Aptitude Battery and Defense Language Proficiency Tests. In a nation of immigrants, this is sound practice, as many soldiers possess heritage language skills.

SF units then deepen cultural fluency via specialized language, culture, terrain, environment, climate, and social-political training. Once qualified as an SF soldier, an individual's particular regional fluency drives assignments. SF teams also remain together for extended periods, fostering unit cohesion and providing the time and experience necessary to develop the functional expertise that complements regional expertise. Another benefit of fewer changes of station is family stability, providing both families and single soldiers with greater opportunities to build long-term relationships that increase personal and professional well-being. This is a retention incentive, allowing the Army to get a greater return on its investment in each soldier.

There is no reason why the larger Army cannot scale several of the SF's regional talent management practices to the larger force. In fact, a recent, multi-year officer talent management pilot program demonstrated how effectively this can be done. In 2010, the Commanding General of the Training and Doctrine Command (TRADOC) and the Assistant Secretary of the Army for Manpower and Reserve Affairs jointly directed the piloting of an officer talent management information system called "Green Pages."[22]

Green Pages was constructed with a talent marketplace at its center, a mechanism that was key to the system's piloting success. While better talent matches were a significant side benefit, the purpose of the pilot was to capture accurate, granular, and timely information on every officer and every duty position, facilitating the **future** management of each. Officers in the reassignment window built personal profiles and provided information, heavily augmenting their official files, while units with pending vacancies simultaneously built job profiles, detailing the specific talents needed to excel in each officer position. Participating officers reviewed job vacancies and expressed preferences for them, while units reviewed available officers and expressed their preferences as well.

As officers and units expressed preferences and communicated directly with one another, preferences on both sides of the market shifted, often dramatically. Units reordered their officer selections and officers reordered their unit choices. In fact, **half** of all participating officers changed their initial assignment preference while exploring the job market. What happened was simple. Units clearly signaled their labor needs, and officers who could meet them were attracted accordingly. Conversely, officers revealed hidden talents, and units who might not have otherwise considered them suddenly took notice. Green Pages also revealed deeper expertise as well. As Figure 1 shows, for example, hidden within this same pilot population were 78 professional engineer certifications that would conservatively cost $16 million to produce.[23]

78 of our 730 Engineers (11% of the Pilot Population) Revealed over $16 Million in Hidden Certifications

Certification	Freq.	Estimated Cost	Savings
American Welding Society (AWS)	1	$10,000	$10,000
Automotive Service Excellence	1	$2,000	$2,000
Certified Facility Manager	2	$10,000	$20,000
Certified Professional Engineer	1	$250,000	$250,000
Certified Project Manager	15	$100,000	$1,500,000
Engineer In Training	51	$250,000	$12,750,000
PE Civil	3	$250,000	$750,000
PE Environmental	3	$250,000	$750,000
Professional Geologist	1	$250,000	$250,000
Total	78*		$16,282,000

Figure 1. Green Pages Revealed over $16M in Certifications.

As Figure 2 indicates, Green Pages pilot results are also germane to the Army's regional alignment efforts. Of the 870 officers in the pilot, official Army data bases, such as the Total Army Personnel Data Base (TAPDB), revealed cultural fluencies spanning just 28 percent of the globe. Yet Green Pages revealed additional fluencies spanning 72 percent of the world, everything from advanced language skills to study abroad, religious or humanitarian missions, official temporary duty, military-to-military exchanges, extended leisure travel, familial connections, etc. HRC then used the granular talent data gathered by Green Pages to optimize officer assignments to the mutual benefit of both individuals and organizations. Scaled across the force, a tool such as Green Pages would be a critical enabler to the Army's regional alignment efforts, provided it was accompanied by appropriate policy changes.

TAPDB Data: 28% of Countries   TAPDB + GP Data: 72% of Countries

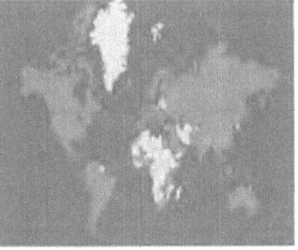

Enhancing Cultural Information Through Green Pages									
		Profile in TAPDB				Profile in Green Pages			
	Total	Officers with Travel	Unique Countries	Officers with Language	Unique Languages	Officers with a New Country	Unique Countries (New)	Officers with a New Language	Unique Languages (New)
EN CPT	435	425	28	40	18	166	79	81	18
EN FG	295	293	42	33	13	97	61	36	11
FA59	81	80	110	9	48	49	58	28	42
Maj AGCCC	50	50	12	6	8	31	32	16	5
Total	870	648	54	58	25	343	39	190	22

Figure 2. Army Green Pages Pilot Cultural Fluency Data.

Create Enduring Human Relationships between Particular Units and Regions.

When describing the complex operational environment, the *Army Strategic Planning Guidance* outlines three Army requirements extending beyond the threat environment. They are: shape relationships with non-hostile rivals, avoiding misunderstandings that could escalate to conflict; partner with friends and allies to create favorable regional conditions (social, economic, political, military, etc.); and work with developing states to prevent disorder that could escalate to major combat operations or strategic strike options.[24] Success in each of these depends heavily upon mature, trusting, and **enduring** human relationships. In fact, the Army believes that such relationships □ . . play a critical role in shaping the strategic environment.□[25]

Enduring human relations must be nurtured between an organization and the population it operates in or around. Consider a sports franchise, for example. Yankees fans are not just enamored with pinstripes or the iconic, interlocking □NY□ logo. First and foremost, they feel a special relationship to the team because of its abundance of enduring stars. Across the decades, they have become familiar with Babe Ruth, Lou Gehrig, Joe DiMaggio, Mickey Mantle, and Derek Jeter. They feel that they □know□ these men, even though not personally acquainted with them. If, however, the Yankees were nothing but a collection of journeyman ballplayers that came and went annually, the public's affinity for the team would be significantly diminished.

By the same token, the Army□ Soldiers need time to build strong interpersonal relationships with regional populations, to represent more than a shoulder patch or unit guidon. During the recent wars in Iraq and Afghanistan, for example, one of the most daunting challenges for a newly deployed brigade combat team (BCT) was establishing effective relationships with local tribes, governments, police, military leaders, and their own higher headquarters. Although the previous BCT had cultivated and nurtured these relationships, each newly deployed brigade had to start building its own relationships from scratch.

As already discussed, SF regional alignment policies significantly ameliorate these challenges. The Army National Guard (ARNG) provides another example of effective, long-term partnering to produce enduring human relationships. For over 20 years, the National Guard State Partnership Program (NGSPP) has successfully developed 65 unique security partnerships involving 71 nations worldwide.[26] The success of this program is due in large part to the fact that there is little personnel change within ARNG units. When these units deploy to conduct partnership activities, the same soldiers work with the host nation᾿s military personnel, who develop an affinity for the ARNG unit because it is more than a patch￱ it is people.

Simultaneously, low personnel churn allows these ARNG units to build deep regional expertise through cultural immersion during repeated deployments to the same country. As Major General Rick Waddell, Deputy Commanding General for Mobilization and Reserve Affairs for U.S. Southern Command, recently observed, ￱These [ARNG Soldiers] . . . stick around for a long time, and long-term relationships may pay off in unforeseen circumstances in the future.￱[27]

While there are fundamental differences between Regular Army and ARNG units, active component regional alignment could readily adopt some of the practices that make the NGSPP so successful. Wartime conditions may have made it impossible to deploy units for multiyear tours, but peacetime conditions in many regions afford the Army with opportunities to increase soldier assignment length, reducing the personnel churn so destructive to establishing and maintaining enduring human relationships.

Redesign the Army Force Generation Model.

Through the three phases of today's ARFORGEN Model cycle, modularity calls for "locking down" the population of each BCT as it moves from the "train/ ready" force pool to the "available" force pool. The intent is to enhance unit cohesion and operational effectiveness during deployment.[28] Redeployment then shatters that cohesion as soldiers move en masse to their next assignments. Instead of the incremental personnel churn that allows units to retain a modicum of institutional memory and regional expertise, current ARFORGEN practices create "all or nothing" units whipsawing in and out of the proverbial "band of excellence." While the integrative efforts of joint and Army component commands offset this to an extent, they, too, are challenged to build and maintain regional expertise and relationships due to personnel churn within their own headquarters.

ARFORGEN fails to appreciate that despite standardization, each BCT is a unique collection of individuals. Its outsized focus upon "plug and play" interchangeability fails to leverage that uniqueness. As a result, ARFORGEN is ill-suited to producing stable, culturally fluent, mission-tailored forces to meet regional challenges.[29] According to the *Army Strategic*

Planning Guidance, deployment by BCT is likely to become a thing of the past anyway, as regionally aligned forces are organized into ⬜squad to Corps-sized formations empowered by soldiers.⬜[30]

For example, the entire 2nd BCT, First Infantry Division, did not deploy to Africa. Instead, this "first" regionally aligned brigade deployed one infantry battalion to execute split-based operations in multiple locations, thousands of miles apart.[31] Despite this, the battalion⬜s standardized pre-deployment training was identical to that of its parent BCT and that of non-Africa aligned BCTs.[32]

Two lessons emerge from this example. First, modular brigades should no longer be the centerpiece of the force generation model, at least not in peacetime. The Army should recognize that smaller teams are more likely to be called upon to meet regional challenges. Second, certain sub-units required a higher level of regional expertise than others, and within those smaller teams, certain individuals needed deeper expertise as well. In other words, a unit can become fundamentally more effective in region-specific missions if leavened with genuine regional experts who are afforded extensive tenure, regionally focused civilian or professional military education, and recurring regional assignments. Given that smaller elements within the BCT⬜ or, ⬜teams within teams⬜ will have unique mission requirements for regional alignment, the Army should liberalize the ARFORGEN cycle to man, train, and resource each of these teams according to its specific mission requirements.

To create sound human relationships and deepen regional expertise, the Army must redesign its force generation model, particularly its personnel component, in four ways. First, command teams, intelligence, operations and logistics staffs, and special staff such as chaplains, staff judge advocates, and civil affairs or medical personnel are more likely to require regional fluency than other unit members. They represent the ⌐front facing⌐ part of the unit that interacts most extensively with regional partners. These teams requiring regional expertise will require more time to train than those teams with a primarily functional mission, which may only require regional familiarity and can acquire it within a shorter amount of time.

Next, the Army must assign personnel to teams that either possess regional expertise or have the potential to develop it. With talent management, the Army can "see" language proficiency and aptitude, cultural fluency, pertinent academic qualifications, and functional specialties pertinent to the mission-tailored requirements of the region. To build effective teams, regionally oriented skills and skill levels can be combined in a manner that can facilitate professional development for all team members.

Third, the Army must allow regional experts time to deepen their expertise before arriving at a unit. This may involve 6 months to 1 year spent conducting language training or advanced civil schooling. Talent management will also help the Army select the most appropriate candidates for these advanced training opportunities. Intensive regional training prior to arrival at the unit provides the commander with trained and ready regional **and** functional experts.

Finally, the Army must lengthen the time for which personnel with regional expertise are assigned to units. By extending the amount of time regional experts are assigned to a unit, commanders will have at their disposal deeper regional knowledge and experience that will serve the unit well beyond just one ARFORGEN or one and a half cycles. Arrival and departure times for regional experts must be carefully managed to prevent the movement of trained regional experts at the same time. Different timelines for different teams allow the brigade to be constantly ready, regardless of the phase of the ARFORGEN cycle in which functional teams may be. With a critical mass of regional experts constantly resident within the unit, the more rapid arrival and departure of functional experts will have less of an effect on overall brigade readiness.

Maintain the Global ⌐Flex⌐ Capabilities of Regionally Aligned Units.

As the nation⌐s principal land force:

> . . . the Army is globally responsive and regionally-aligned; it is an indispensible partner and provider of a full range of capabilities to combatant commanders in a Joint, interagency, intergovernmental and multi-national environment.[33]

Regionally aligned units cannot allow their core competencies to atrophy. In other words, **over** specialization could leave the Army unable to respond to unforeseen contingencies. The pace of global change and the ambiguity the global threat environment may demand units to rapidly pivot from one region to another and from one mission set to another.[34]

Consider that the greatest number of BCTs are regionally aligned to the Middle East, yet these units should be able to perform in the Pacific region, particularly if leavened with the appropriate experts. This is not unlike the Army⌐s experience in World War II. After defeating Germany, dozens of Army divisions in Europe began preparation for the invasion of Japan, and hundreds of officers and soldiers from the Pacific theater were rapidly transferred to these units to prepare them for new terrain and a new adversary. While the use of the atom bomb halted these preparations, they nonetheless provide an excellent lesson.

Within its overarching regional alignment plan, the Army should also try to anticipate the size and duration of certain contingencies and develop three corresponding response packages: small/short-term, small/long-term, and large/any term.

For small/short-term contingencies, forces already aligned to the region should be sufficient. Initial alignment plans have allocated forces based on the projected prevent-shape-win requirements of each theater. Ideally, with the expertise gained from deployment planning, training, and sustainment coordination for multiple engagement missions, teams within the aligned brigade(s) are at the highest level of readiness to respond to the contingency.

When faced with small contingencies of longer duration, the Army should establish a rotation system for elements of brigades aligned to that region. Much like the SF Group rotations during Operation IRAQI FREEDOM and Operation ENDURING FREEDOM, right-sized, regionally expert teams can rotate in and out of the contingency zone, providing a sustainable flow of forces to appropriately resource the mission.

Last, for major regional contingencies (MRC) requiring more forces than are aligned to a region, the Army will need to quickly redirect brigades from other regions. In this case, forces aligned outside the contingency region should form the MRC's strategic reserve. Regionally expert units should also train these units prior to their employment, and again during reception, staging, and onward integration activities in theater.

CONCLUSIONS

In a recent memo to the service chiefs and combatant commanders, Chairman of the Joint Chiefs General Martin Dempsey expressed his desire to provide commanders with ⬜deep regional expertise to execute their missions, starting in the Phase 0 shaping environment.⬜[35] He then said that today, such ⬜deep regional expertise exists [only] by chance.⬜With this in mind, and facing a strategic pivot to the Pacific, the Chairman has called for the creation of an "Asia-Pacific Hands" program to build a ⬜deep bench⬜of regionally expert flag officers. While this might redress a perceived expertise shortage in one corner of the globe, it neglects the rest of the world and cannot assure that newly created Pacific experts will actually be employed to good effect.

For **any** regional alignment efforts to yield fruit, the Army must first overhaul its industrial age personnel management system. It must recognize the unique talents possessed by each of its soldiers. The Army must then move toward an information age talent management paradigm, enhancing its abilities to build units with genuine regional expertise. Simultaneously, it must redesign its force generation model, providing an increased share of soldier with the ongoing education and regional tenure required to promote enduring human relationships with regional partners.

Perhaps most importantly, in order for the Army to truly ⬜prevent, shape, and win,⬜ it must maintain its ability to respond to contingencies around the globe. Regionally tailored doctrine, equipment, organization, and intelligence are only part of the solution. Appropriately expert human capital is the lynchpin to regional success, and only a genuine talent management system can provide it.

ENDNOTES

1. North Atlantic Treaty, Brussels, Belgium: The North Atlantic Treaty Organization, available from *www.nato.int/cps/en/natolive/official_texts_17120.htm*. The Army's current posture on the Korean Peninsula mirrors this practice, albeit on a smaller scale than being proposed by the Army today.

2. General Raymond Odierno, Regionally-aligned Forces: A New Model for Building Partnerships, *Army Live*, The Official Blog of the United States Army, March 22, 2012, available from *armylive.dodlive.mil/index.php/2012/03/aligned-forces/*.

3. *Army Strategic Planning Guidance 2013*, Washington, DC: Department of the Army, 2013, p. 4, available from *usarmy.vo.llnwd. net/e2/rv5_downloads/info/references/army_strategic_planning_ guidance.pdf*. Italics are the authors'

4. Gary Sheftick, ARCENT Says Future Hinges on Regional Alignments, *www.Army.mil*: The Official Homepage of the United States Army, October 28, 2013, available from *www.army.mil/ article/114027/*.

5. *Army Strategic Planning Guidance 2013*, p. 5.

6. The Regionally Aligned Force Concept explicitly acknowledges that the forces will be regionally aligned, mission tailored force organized by leaders into squad- to corps-sized formations empowered by Soldiers. [Emphasis added.] *Army Strategic Planning Guidance 2013*, p. 5.

7. John Vandiver, AFRICOM First to Test New Regional Brigade Concept, *Stripes.com*, May 17, 2012, available from *www.stripes.com/news/africom-first-to-test-new-regional-brigade-concept-1.177476*.

8. Antonieta Rico, New Training to Focus on Regionally-aligned Forces Concept, *Defense News*, October 23,

2013, available from *www.defensenews.com/article/20131023/ SHOWSCOUT/310230019/New-Training-Focus-Regionally-Aligned-Forces-Concept.*

9. Lance M. Bacon, ⊓Regional Alignment May Boost Soldiers⊓ Career Stability,⊓*Army Times Online,* December 10, 2013, available from *www.armytimes.com/article/20131210/CAREERS/312100016/ Regional alignment-may-boost-soldiers-career-stability.*

10. *The U.S. Army Capstone Concept: Training and Doctrine Command (TRADOC) Pamphlet (PAM) 525-3-0,* Fort Eustis, VA: TRADOC, 2012, p. 18, available from *www.tradoc.army.mil/tpubs/pams/ tp525-3-0.pdf.*

11. *Ibid.*

12. Casey Wardynski, David S. Lyle, and Michael J. Colarusso, *Talent: Implications for a U.S. Army Officer Corps Strategy,* Carlisle, PA: Strategic Studies Institute U.S. Army War College, 2009, p. 5, available from *www.strategicstudiesinstitute.army.mil/pubs/display. cfm?pubID=948.*

13. Expressing rank as a measure of experience within a given functional specialty is, in fact, an inaccuracy since officers can move between branches and still maintain their rank. In this sense, rank does not measure functional expertise in all cases, and becomes an even more arbitrary metric for how an individual should be employed.

14. Paul Peters, interview by Raven Bukowski, West Point, NY, February 5, 2014. This example is one of hundreds that we uncovered during our research and seems to be the impetus for recent articles bemoaning the loss of talent from the Army⊓s officer ranks.

15. *Ibid.*

16. Wardynski, Lyle, and Colarusso, *Talent: Implications for a U.S. Army Officer Corps Strategy.*

17. *Army Strategic Planning Guidance 2013,* p. 10.

18. *The U.S. Army Capstone Concept: Training and Doctrine Command Pamphlet*, p. 34.

19. This number includes all Soldiers who were assessed into the military between 1991 and 2000 and is generated from the TAPDB. Office of Economic and Manpower Analysis, "All Soldiers Re-deployed to Korea as a Percentage of those Deployed Once 1991-2000,☐ Total Army Personnel Data Base, February 20, 2014.

20. Jim Garamone, ☐Three-Year Korea Tours Good for Soldiers, Alliance, Commander Says,☐ *American Forces Press Service*, March 23, 2009, available from *www.defense.gov/News/NewsArticle.aspx?ID=53601.*

21. *2013 Academic Handbook*, Fort Bragg, NC: U.S. Army John F. Kennedy Special Warfare Center and School, 2013, p. 28, available from *www.soc.mil/swcs/_pdf/AcademicHandbook.pdf.*

22. *Army Green Pages: Proof-of-Concept Pilot Report*, West Point, NY: Office of Economic and Manpower Analysis, 2012, p. 2.

23. *Army Green Pages: Proof-of-Concept Pilot Report*, pp. 24-26.

24. *Army Strategic Planning Guidance 2013*, p. 3.

25. *Ibid.*, p. 5.

26. ☐The National Guard State Partnership Program,☐ Washington, DC: U.S. National Guard, available from *www.nationalguard.mil/Leadership/JointStaff/J5/InternationalAffairs Division/StatePartnershipProgram.aspx.*

27. Major General Rick Waddell, ☐Remarks to National Security Seminar Students,☐ classroom discussion, National Security Seminar, West Point, NY, February 27, 2014.

28. *Field Manual Interim (FMI) 3-0.1: The Modular Force*, Washington, DC: Headquarters, Department of the Army, January 28, 2008, p. 2-2, available from *fas.org/irp/doddir/army/fmi3-0-1.pdf.*

29. Over time, Army forces will not only be regionally aligned, but "mission-tailored," which means forces are not only proficient in the fundamentals of unified land operations, but also possess specific capabilities tailored for one or more of the 10 missions specified in the *Army Strategic Planning Guidance*. These missions span the range of military operations and include power projection, the deterrence and defeat of aggression, countering weapons of mass destruction, providing a stabilizing presence, disaster relief, and operating effectively in cyberspace. The Army, as part of the joint force, must provide the land component forces necessary to accomplish each of these missions.

30. *Army Strategic Planning Guidance 2013*, p. 5.

31. Lieutenant Colonel Chris Danbeck, phone interview by Major Raven Bukowski, September 5, 2013.

32. Prior to deployment, the 2nd Brigade of the 1st Infantry Division created a partnership with Kansas State University that provided Soldiers with 3 weeks of country-specific classroom training. *Ibid.*

33. *Army Strategic Planning Guidance 2013*, p. 2.

34. Department of the Army G3/5/7, *Regional Alignment of Forces*, PowerPoint Presentation, Washington, DC: U.S. Department of the Army, September 10, 2013, p. 5.

35. General Martin Dempsey, "Asia-Pacific Hands Program: CM-0301-13,☐ memorandum for Chiefs of the Military Services and Commanders of Combatant Commands, December 5, 2013.

U.S. ARMY WAR COLLEGE

Major General William E. Rapp
Commandant

*****

STRATEGIC STUDIES INSTITUTE
and
U.S. ARMY WAR COLLEGE PRESS

Director
Professor Douglas C. Lovelace, Jr.

Director of Research
Dr. Steven K. Metz

Authors
Major Raven Bukowski
Major John Childress
Lieutenant Colonel (Ret.) Michael J. Colarusso
Lieutenant Colonel David S. Lyle

Editor for Production
Dr. James G. Pierce

Publications Assistant
Ms. Rita A. Rummel

*****

Composition
Mrs. Jennifer E. Nevil

www.ingramcontent.com/pod-product-compliance
Lightning Source LLC
Chambersburg PA
CBHW050353290526
45785CB00006B/2754